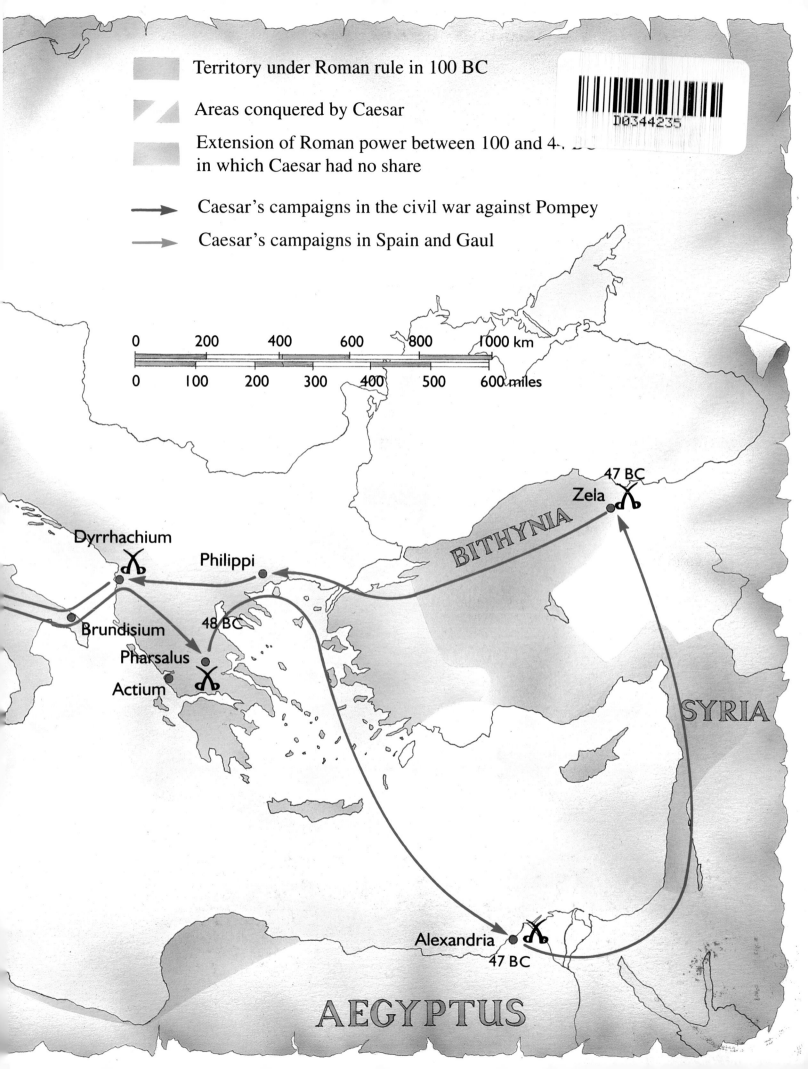

Territory under Roman rule in 100 BC

Areas conquered by Caesar

Extension of Roman power between 100 and 4.. ..
in which Caesar had no share

Caesar's campaigns in the civil war against Pompey

Caesar's campaigns in Spain and Gaul

Dyrrhachium

Philippi

Zela

47 BC

BITHYNIA

Brundisium

48 BC

Pharsalus

Actium

SYRIA

Alexandria

47 BC

AEGYPTUS

937

# WHO WAS
# JULIUS CAESAR?

## AIDAN WARLOW

### ILLUSTRATED BY CHRIS MOLAN

First published in Great Britain 1997 by
Macdonald Young Books an imprint of
Wayland Books Ltd
61 Western Road
Hove
East Sussex BN3 1JD

Find Wayland on the internet at:
http://www.wayland.co.uk

Series concept and text
© Wendy and Sally Knowles

Design and illustrations
© Macdonald Young Books

Edited by Wendy Knowles
Designed by David Fordham

Printed and bound in
Typeset by Stylize

ISBN 07500 2268 X

Photograph acknowledgements:

We are grateful to the following for permission
to reproduce photographs:
Front cover: Michael Holford, (tl); © Michael
Holford/Collection The British Museum (tr);
Ronald Sheridan/Ancient Art & Architecture
Collection, (bl) and (br).

Archivi Alinari, Firenze, page 39(bl);
The Bridgeman Art Library/Verulanium
Museum, St Albans, Hertfordshire, page 19(t);
The Bridgeman Art Library/Louvre, Paris,
page 22(t); The British Museum, London,
pages 25(bl), 28(tl), 28(bl), 30(r); Peter Clayton,
pages 161, 19(c), 35(t), 39(br); C. M. Dixon,
pages 13(l) and 13(br) (Munich Glyptothek),
22(b), 27(tr), 27(br), 32(bl), 41; English
Heritage Photographic Library, page 27(bl);
© Michael Holford/Collection The British
Museum, London, pages 10(r), 13(tr), 14(l),
14(r), 16(r), 20, 32(br), 35(bl); Michael Holford,
21, 34; National Trust Photographic Library,
page 40 (Paul Mulcahy); Ronald Sheridan/
Ancient Art & Architecture Collection, pages 9,
10(l), 15, 16(c), 17, 19(b), 25(tl), 28(tr), 30(l),
32(t), 35(br), 36(t), 36(b), 39(t).

Picture research by Valerie Mulcahy

# CONTENTS

# CAESAR'S ROME

Julius Caesar is regarded as one of the greatest generals of all time. An outstanding political leader, renowned for his ruthlessness and efficiency, he defeated all his opponents to become Dictator of Rome. However, fears that he would make himself king prompted his murder in 44BC and resulted in major changes in the way the Roman empire was governed.

*In the centre of Rome was the forum or market place which was always crowded and busy. Around the forum were the main temples, palaces, government offices and law courts. The Colosseum was completed about a century later.*

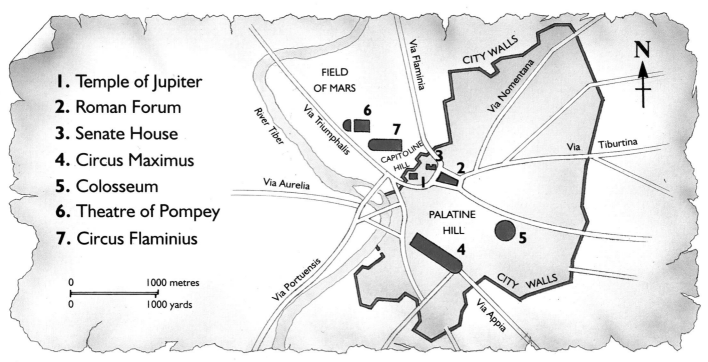

1. Temple of Jupiter
2. Roman Forum
3. Senate House
4. Circus Maximus
5. Colosseum
6. Theatre of Pompey
7. Circus Flaminius

## WHO WERE THE ROMANS?

The earliest Romans were tough tribesmen living in the area of Latium in western Italy. They built a city, Rome, ruled by kings, on the banks of the River Tiber – according to tradition in the year 753 BC. Gradually Rome conquered all the neighbouring cities and tribes until it had gained control of the whole of Italy and had begun its conquest abroad. By the time of Julius Caesar, Rome controlled most of the Mediterranean and was a bustling city of more than a million people.

*Roman society consisted of four separate groups of people:*

*The PATRICIANS, a small circle of rich and powerful upper-class families.*
*The EQUITES, who were the wealthy bankers and business people.*
*The PLEBEIANS, who were the ordinary working people.*

*Finally there were the SLAVES who could be bought and sold in the market and did all the worst jobs.*

*Roman senators. The Senate was a law-making body of about 300 important and respected citizens, most of whom had themselves held senior government posts.*

*Caesar was probably typically Mediterranean looking with dark hair and brown eyes.*

### HOW WAS ROME GOVERNED?

The Romans had hated their kings and had expelled the last one in 510 BC. In their place they introduced the Republic, a form of government in which the people voted in their own rulers. All important officials had to be voted into office by the citizens at one of their big public meetings called an assembly. To make sure that even the elected leaders did not become too powerful, they could only hold office for one year.

### WAS THIS SYSTEM OF GOVERNMENT WORKING WELL?

No. When Caesar was a child, the system was already breaking down. Politicians had become less honest and used bribery and threats to persuade people to vote for them. The poorer people felt exploited by the greedy rich. And rivalry for power among political leaders led to a period of open warfare in 91-88 BC known as the Social War. This is the background against which the young Julius Caesar grew up.

# BEGINNINGS

Gaius Julius Caesar was born in July, 102 BC. Julius was his family or clan name. He would have been called Gaius by his family and friends and Caesar later on. He had two sisters.

*It is said that he had to be cut out of his mother Aurelia's womb. We still refer to this form of childbirth as a Caesarean Operation.*

*A household god or Lar. The Lares were the spirits of dead ancestors who were supposed to guard the home.*

*Roman families tended to be small with three children or less. Caesar's parents would have been glad to have had a son because only a son could carry on the Julian family name.*

**WHAT SORT OF FAMILY DID HE COME FROM?**

The Julian family were patricians, though not so rich as some. Caesar's father was also called Gaius Julius Caesar. He had himself held a minor government post and moved in high political circles. More importantly, Caesar's aunt Julia was married to the greatest Roman leader of his day, General Marius, the leader of the Plebian or People's Party. He led an army in the Social War and ruled Rome as consul for 7 years.

*Upper class Romans loved good food and would spend enormous sums of money on it. Most of their food was similar to our own. But they also enjoyed more elaborate dishes: stuffed dormice, ostrich steaks, roast peacock. One family is said to have served a wild boar stuffed with live birds!*

## WHERE DID THEY LIVE?

It would probably have been a large town house with mosaic floors, painted walls and a courtyard with a pool and a fountain. There would not have been much furniture. Patricians such as the Julians, usually had a house in the country as well. They owned farm land and often made a great deal of money supplying food to the cities.

## WHAT WOULD LIFE HAVE BEEN LIKE IN THE JULIAN HOUSEHOLD?

Life would have been very comfortable. Slaves did all the work in the house and on the estates. They also looked after the children. But the men in the Julian family were not lazy. As patricians they would have been expected to take on important jobs as judges, soldiers and officials.

*Caesar's mother, Aurelia, would have been responsible for the smooth running of her large household and supervising the education of her three children.*

# CAESAR'S CHILDHOOD

As the son of a patrician, Caesar's whole childhood would have been a preparation for a life in politics, law or public speaking. From an early age he would have been encouraged to learn from his father and been allowed to sit in on his father's discussions with friends and clients.

**DID HE GO TO SCHOOL?**

Caesar's parents were far too grand to send him to an ordinary school. They hired a private tutor, a former slave called Gnipho, to give him lessons. Gnipho taught Caesar to read and write in his own language of Latin and he taught him Greek. He also taught him rhetoric which meant making up speeches on different subjects and delivering them in front of an audience.

*Young Caesar loved writing. Later on he wrote a famous book about the Gallic Wars.*

## WAS HE A GOOD PUPIL?

The young Caesar worked hard and was specially good at writing and rhetoric. His parents were proud of him but they were also strict. He would be severely beaten by his father if he stepped out of line – and was never allowed to cry.

*A Roman inkpot and pen. Caesar's famous war commentaries would probably have been written with pen and ink on papyrus scrolls.*

## WHAT ELSE DID HE LEARN?

Like all patrician boys, Caesar learnt to ride a horse. Probably his father taught him when they visited their country house. He was a good rider as a boy and trained himself to ride at a fast trot with his hands behind his back. He also learnt to swim, which saved his life as a soldier later on in Egypt.

*Caesar's uncle, Marius (right), the leader of the Plebian Party.*

*Two of Caesar's uncles were murdered on the orders of Sulla (left), the leader of the Patrician Party.*

## DID ANYTHING IMPORTANT HAPPEN TO HIM AS A CHILD?

When Caesar was only fifteen, his father was going for a walk, stopped to tie up his shoelace – and suddenly died. It was not a good time to lose a father. There was a vicious civil war, known as the Social War going on between Caesar's own uncle, Marius and his great rival, Sulla, the leader of the Patrician Party, for control of Rome. With the death of his father, Caesar was now the head of the Julian household. It was an unpleasant introduction to adult life.

# THE GROWN-UP CAESAR

He clearly saw himself as a very special person. The story goes that when he was young he had a magnificent horse with very odd hooves which were divided into five sections like five fingers. Fortune tellers said that the owner of this amazing horse would one day rule the world! Only Caesar ever rode it. Years later he had a statue of it erected in his new forum in Rome.

**WHAT DID HE LOOK LIKE?**

The many stone statues or busts of Caesar that have survived show him to have had a sharp, thin face – definitely handsome and very alert-looking. As he grew older he got a bit short of hair and had to brush it forward to cover his baldness.

*Caesar was very fussy about his appearance. Every day an expert barber shaved his face, arranged his hair and plucked out unwanted whiskers with a pair of tweezers. He even had all the hairs removed from his body!*

In Roman times, marriage (left), shown by the clasping of hands often took place for financial or political reasons. Caesar's first marriage was to Cornelia.

On becoming engaged a couple exchanged rings (right).

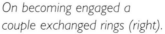

**WAS HE MARRIED?**

He was married three times. His first marriage at sixteen was to Cornelia, the daughter of Sulla's enemy, Cinna, and they had a baby girl called Julia. After Cornelia's death he married a glamorous lady called Pompeia. She was suspected (probably unfairly) of being unfaithful to him and so he divorced her. Finally he married Calpurnia, who cared deeply for him for the remainder of his life. They did not have any children.

*He had a very stylish way of dressing, wearing his tunic belt loosely under his toga in a specially casual way.*

### DID HE ALSO HAVE GIRL FRIENDS?

Yes, far too many! The most famous was Cleopatra, the beautiful Queen of Egypt, whom he met during his war with Pompey *(see page 30)*. She had a son called Caesarion and almost certainly the father was Caesar. Another great love of his life was Servilia whose son, Brutus was later to be one of Caesar's murderers.

*Cleopatra, Queen of Egypt, Caesar's most famous girl friend. They went on a romantic trip up the River Nile. Later on she visited him in Rome.*

### HOW DID HE RELAX?

He loved parties, fine food and pretty women. He was also a great collector of every form of art; jewels, especially freshwater pearls, fine vases and paintings. Not surprisingly he often got into heavy debt. But he was also very serious. Work always came first.

15

# CAESAR, THE YOUNG WARRIOR

By the time of Caesar, Rome controlled most of the Mediterranean. As a result of his uncle, General Marius's reforms, the Republic's boundaries were defended by a large, full-time army that was well-equipped and well-trained. Soldiers were used to conquer new lands, police the provinces and put down rebellions.

**WHAT MADE HIM JOIN THE ARMY?**

Caesar joined the army when he was nineteen with the rank of tribune. It was what every smart young patrician boy did who wanted to hold public office, and Caesar would have been particularly keen. The usual practice was to serve in the army for a year and then join the staff of a governor.

The army offered the excitement of travelling to distant countries that the Romans had conquered – Spain, southern France, North Africa. The tribes in those places didn't always want to be ruled by the Romans and sometimes rebelled. The army would be sent in to keep control.

*A Roman legionary wearing a metal breast plate over a woollen tunic and a helmet of leather or metal. He would have been armed with a short sword, two javelins and a shield.*

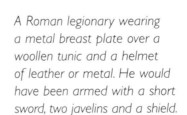

*A legionary's sword had a double-cutting edge and a stabbing point. As a general Caesar liked to reward his men with swords with gold mountings, because he wanted them to look after their equipment.*

Julius Caesar was sent to fight a war in the East. Unlike most sons of great families who were attached to the staff of a general or governor, Caesar took his military duties seriously and fought in the front line. He quickly showed outstanding military skills and was given an oak leaf crown for his bravery.

As a junior officer, Caesar learnt how to fight in tough conditions, how to lead other men and how to win their respect. It was a good training for the future.

After three years he decided to return to Rome. The dictator, Sulla, who had confiscated Caesar's inheritance and tried to make him divorce his wife, Cornelia, was now dead. Times had changed. Caesar wanted power. You had to be in Rome to get that.

## WAS HE A GOOD SOLDIER?

*Soldiers building a fort. Once they had established a far-flung empire, the Romans were faced with the enormous problem of guarding it.*

*On one occasion he saved the life of another officer when they were attacking the Greek walled city of Mytilene and was given an oak leaf crown.*

# KIDNAPPED BY PIRATES!

Shortly after leaving the army, Caesar had an exciting adventure. He was travelling along the Greek coast when his ship was surrounded by a group of strange boats. They belonged to pirates.

The pirates drew up close to Caesar's ship and jumped aboard. There was a furious battle. Quickly the pirates gained control and held Caesar prisoner. Realising that he was an important Roman citizen, travelling with his own doctor and two personal servants, they took all Caesar's money – and then said that he would be released only if his friends on land sent twenty silver coins in ransom money.

*Pirates were a menace throughout the Mediterranean, attacking and robbing not only ships, but towns and whole regions. Their ships were very seaworthy and well-equipped.*

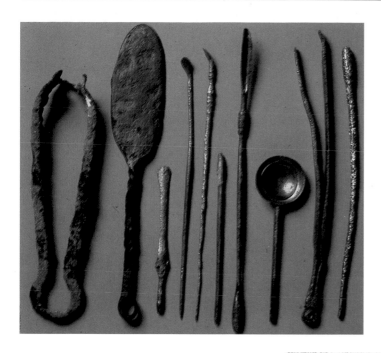

*Roman iron and bronze medical instruments – the Romans gained most of their medical knowledge from the Greeks. Most wealthy Romans had their own doctor.*

## WAS HE AFRAID?

No. He laughed at the pirates' ransom request. "Twenty silver coins only? I'm worth a lot more than that! They'll pay fifty to set me free!" The pirates were delighted. Messengers were sent off to get the money and meanwhile Caesar was locked up in a cabin with his doctor and their two servants. Caesar was totally unafraid. "When I'm free, I'll have you all crucified!" he joked.

For thirty-eight days he was kept prisoner. He amused himself by insulting the pirates. He also wrote poems and speeches which he recited to them; when they weren't impressed he called them idiots.

*Clumsy merchant ships such as these, shown in this floor mosaic from Ostia, would have been an easy prey for swift pirate galleys.*

## HOW DID HE DEAL WITH THE PIRATES?

Eventually the messengers came back with the ransom money of fifty silver talents and the pirates happily released Caesar. They must have thought that they had seen the last of him. Once safely on land, he quickly organised a Roman fighting ship and came back to attack the pirates. He not only recaptured the ransom money, he also destroyed the pirates' stronghold and captured the rest of their loot. And then he had all the pirates crucified.

*The Roman navy used fighting ships, (shown on this coin above), manned by professionally trained sailors rather than slaves, to patrol the sea against pirates.*

# PUSHING HIS WAY INTO POWER

Safely back in Rome, Caesar planned how to move into a position of power. To get an important job, you needed to persuade people to vote for you in the assembly. Caesar knew how to do this. Like most ambitious Romans, he bribed people to vote for him. Sometimes he would bully them. Sometimes he would do deals, offering jobs to friends if they would give him what he wanted.

A Roman consul. As consul Caesar was in charge of the army in Rome and had control over most government departments.

### WHAT JOBS DID HE DO?

Quaestor was his first big job. This put him in charge of taxes and public money. Aedile was his next appointment. This involved organising public sporting events, such as chariot races, which helped to make him popular. A job as praetor or judge followed. By this time Caesar had spent so much money on bribery and expensive living that he was heavily in debt. He went off to Spain for a while to be the governor of a province. There he made a lot of money for himself by seizing treasure from the local tribes. Finally, for one year only, he was given a very high job as a consul.

*Caesar was renowned for his ability to dictate four important letters to his scribes simultaneously, and as many as seven unimportant ones!*

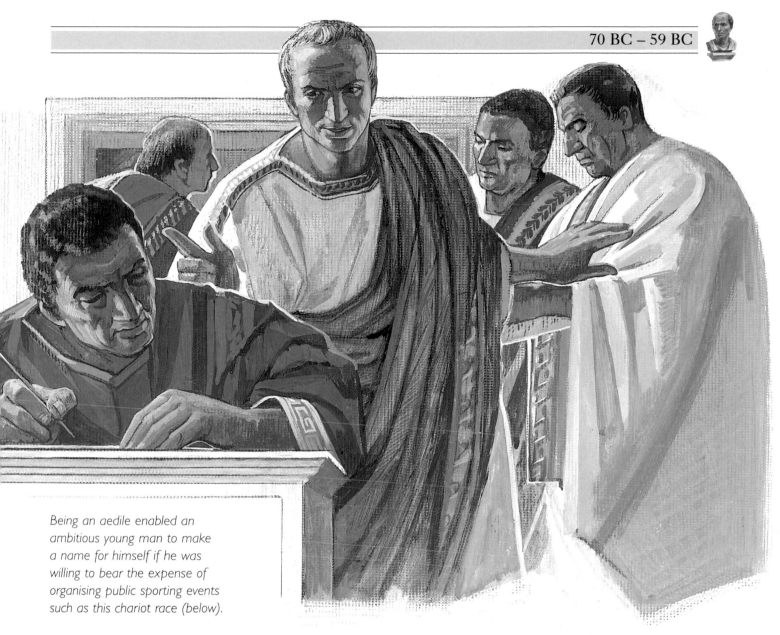

Being an aedile enabled an ambitious young man to make a name for himself if he was willing to bear the expense of organising public sporting events such as this chariot race (below).

Like most ambitous Roman politicians Caesar (above) bribed people or did deals with them to get them to vote for him.

## WAS HE GOOD AT THESE JOBS?

He might have used crooked methods to get elected – but once he was there he carried them out extremely well. Everybody admired the way he told people what to do. He always knew what was going on. He didn't make mistakes. But Caesar still wasn't at the very top. He longed to be the one man in command of *everybody*.

# GAINING POPULARITY WITH THE MOB

To get on in Roman politics, you had to persuade the ordinary people to vote for you at the annual elections. By fair means or foul, you had to win popularity. The majority of voters were simple people who could be attracted to any leader who offered a bit of glamour and crude entertainment.

**HOW DID CAESAR WIN POPULARITY?**

One way to become popular was to organise gladiator fights. These were revolting displays of blood and violence but the Romans thought they were marvellous. Rich men such as Caesar hired and trained large numbers of gladiators and then invited the public to watch them fight – at no cost.

*Gladiator's helmet. Caesar dressed his gladiators in silver armour to draw extra attention to them.*

**WHO WERE THE GLADIATORS?**

Sometimes the gladiators were criminals whose only way of escaping execution was to fight in public. Others were foreigners who had been captured in war. Hardly any of them wanted to be gladiators. They fought to the death – which meant that an average gladiator did not live for long.

*Gladiators in action (left). Caesar had so many the government was afraid that he would use them as a special army.*

## WASN'T IT A TERRIBLE WASTE OF MONEY?

Yes, all this cost Caesar huge sums of money which is why he got so heavily into debt and had to recover his losses in Spain. But money spent on gladiators was not wasted. The rough citizens of Rome thought Caesar was being kind and generous – and they voted for him in the assembly. His plan was working.

*Sometimes a wounded gladiator would appeal to the spectators to save him. If the crowd pointed their thumbs up, he was allowed to live.*

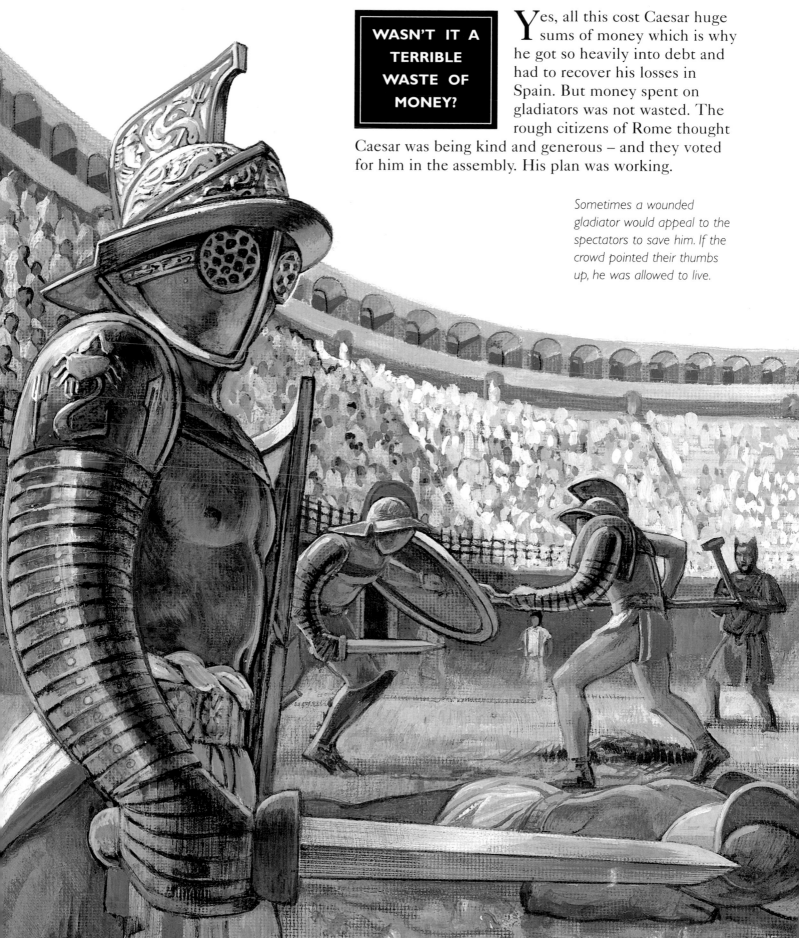

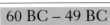

# CONQUERING HERO

Caesar had *almost* got to the top in Rome. He was consul, which was a very powerful job but could only last for one year. He had to share power with two other very strong men called Pompey and Crassus. The three of them ruled together in 60-59 BC calling themselves the Triumvirate.

Then Caesar did a surprising thing. He left Rome altogether and went back to his old career in the army. He spent the next ten years conquering Gaul (modern France) and amassing a great fortune.

*Caesar drilled his men in new tactics and techniques. Here Roman soldiers are using a tortoise formation – holding their shields above their heads, as protection against enemy missiles.*

## WHAT WAS HIS JOB IN THE ARMY?

He was put in command of the army in Gaul (modern France). At that time the Romans ruled only the southern part of Gaul. The central and northern areas were occupied by various native tribes who spent much of their time fighting each other. The situation was made worse by hordes of German tribes invading from the east, led by a very fierce king called Ariovistus. There was also another tribe moving into Gaul from Switzerland called the Helvetii. Caesar made up his mind to drive the Germans out of Gaul and bring the whole area under Roman rule.

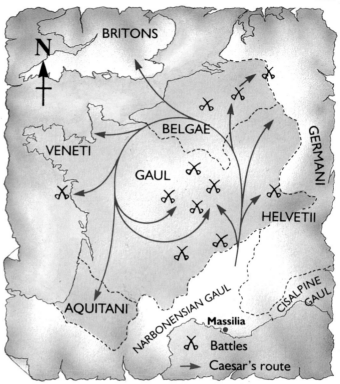

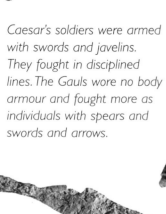

*Caesar's soldiers were armed with swords and javelins. They fought in disciplined lines. The Gauls wore no body armour and fought more as individuals with spears and swords and arrows.*

## DID HE SUCCEED AGAINST THE HELVETII?

Their army outnumbered Caesar's by three to one. Caesar did not attack them at first. He simply followed them for about two weeks, keeping his distance. When they finally decided to attack, Caesar, as always, was ready.

The Romans formed three straight lines along a hillside. The Helvetii charged but the Romans replied by hurling a mass of javelins, killing hundreds of the enemy's front line and throwing them into chaos. Then the Romans charged down the hill with their swords in highly disciplined lines. The Helvetii tried to counter-attack from the side. But Caesar drew his army round in a perfectly controlled movement and advanced on the Helvetii. He destroyed their army and slaughtered their women and children.

Many more battles followed. He won a huge victory over the Germanic tribes and Ariovistus was lucky to escape with a few of his followers back to Germany.

# DID HE EVER LOSE A BATTLE?

No. But he nearly did at least once in 57 BC. One of the bravest tribes to resist Caesar was called the Nervii. The Nervii had sworn to fight the Romans till the last man died.

**WHAT HAPPENED?**

They managed to creep through and attack before the Romans had even time to put on their armour and helmets. For the first time the Romans were in confusion. Caesar had to charge up and down his lines shouting orders to his men to get them into some sort of order. Taking a shield from one of the ordinary soldiers he rode out in front of the army and ordered them to follow him.

He would probably have lost his battle had not another brilliant young officer called Labienus arrived just in time with extra troops to attack the enemy from the rear. Of the 60,000 Nervii who first attacked Caesar, only 500 survived. But this time Caesar did spare their women and children.

## WAS HE REALLY A GREAT GENERAL?

For someone who had almost no previous experience of commanding a large army, he was brilliant. He always watched and judged the enemy's movements carefully, and he was very well organised. When the time was right, he acted with a speed and decisiveness that took everybody by surprise. His troops had complete confidence and respect for him.

*One Roman writer calculated that Caesar's wars had altogether caused the deaths of 1,192,000 people.*

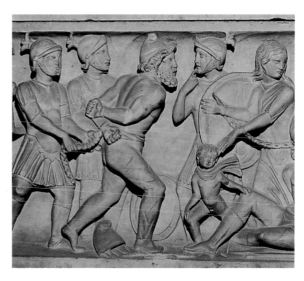

*In Gaul, Caesar had to face brave and dangerous enemies. He was quite ruthless and frequently slaughtered defeated opponents.*

*A soldier's grain measure (above). Caesar attached great importance to regular supplies and provided for his men generously.*

*During particularly fierce fighting (left), Caesar would lead from the front and rally his men.*

## WAS HE RUTHLESS?

He would certainly be called a war criminal today. He committed the most appalling acts of violence in his army career. On one occasion he conquered an area in Eastern France and chopped off the hands of every inhabitant.

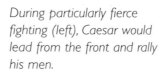

# INVADING BRITAIN

**B**ritain was only a short way across the sea from Gaul. But to the Romans it was a land of mystery. Like most of the Gauls, the tribes living there were Celts – mostly farmers, but also fierce warriors who built large earth fortresses on hillsides to keep their enemies away. The Celts were skilled craftsmen, making beautiful gold and bronze ornaments.

*Roman galley (below). Caesar organised a fleet of 80 galleys and an army of about 20,000 men for his first great invasion of the island of Britain in 55 BC.*

*The back of a Celtic mirror. Most decorated Celtic objects were made of metals such as bronze, iron, gold and silver.*

### WHY DID CAESAR ATTACK BRITAIN?

**P**artly curiosity. He simply wanted to see what it was like and he had heard about the gold. He was also angry with some of the British tribesmen who had been helping his own enemies in Gaul. They needed to be taught a lesson. And of course Caesar always welcomed another chance to win fame and glory.

### HOW DID HE PLAN HIS ATTACK?

**H**e sent an officer called Volusenus over to explore the British coast. But Volusenus only sailed up a short way and never dared to land – so Caesar didn't find out where it was safe.

He organised a fleet of 80 galleys and an army of about 20,000 men for his great invasion. He was confident that this was enough to wipe out a few tribesmen who didn't even wear armour or have strong iron weapons.

*British helmet – Caesar was confident that his army was enough to wipe out a few tribesmen.*

## WHAT WENT WRONG?

Caesar's galleys sailed up the coast of Kent in search of a landing place. The British tribesmen followed on land – knowing every bit of the route. When the Romans finally stopped, they couldn't get their galleys close to the beach. They realised they'd have to wade ashore in their heavy armour.

At first nobody dared jump over the side. Then one brave soldier grabbed his legion's standard and leapt into the water shouting, "Jump, comrades, unless you want to betray our eagle to the enemy!"

The British warriors fought fiercely but were no match for the Romans once they had all come ashore and organised themselves in lines of battle. Wisely the British withdrew on to higher ground and waited for the Romans to make the next move. But there was very little the Romans could do. If they marched inland they had no idea which routes were safe to follow. And the British would carry out vicious hit-and-run attacks which made all movement unsafe.

It took Caesar only four days to realise he'd have to leave Britain. His army was short of food and many of his ships had been damaged in a storm. He had no better luck the second time he invaded Britain in 54 BC.

*At first nobody dared jump, then one brave soldier grabbed his legion's standard and leapt into the water.*

# THE BATTLE FOR POWER

Caesar had proved himself to be a great general. Now he was hungry for political power. He was determined to become supreme and absolute ruler of Rome and its empire. He was willing to wait and plan slowly – but he had to get there in the end.

### WHAT WERE HIS CHANCES OF POWER?

He had a huge well-trained army in Gaul that was completely loyal to him. He was also now immensely rich. It was tempting simply to march on Rome and seize power. One man stood in his way – his great rival, Pompey. Pompey was, like Caesar, a fine general and an experienced politician. More seriously, he was already in Rome in firm control. He had to be eliminated.

A Celtic gold torque – thanks to the hoards of treasure his army had seized in Gaul, Caesar was now very rich.

*Pompey (see coin left) had once been Caesar's friend and happily married to his beloved daughter, Julia. But after Julia died in childbirth, they became rivals and enemies.*

*We still use the expression 'to cross the Rubicon' if we make a decision we can't go back on.*

### WOULD CAESAR GO TO WAR?

A small river stream called the Rubicon divided Gaul from Italy. In 49 BC everybody knew that if Caesar brought his army over the Rubicon into Italy it would mean the outbreak of civil war.

For a while he hesitated. On the final day, he spent the afternoon watching a gladiator fight, later joined some friends for a feast, and then went down alone to stand on the banks of the Rubicon in the dark. Then with the words, 'The die must be cast', he ordered his troops to cross the river.

## HOW WAS THE CIVIL WAR FOUGHT?

To begin with Pompey fled from Rome and Caesar quickly marched in to take control. But Pompey still had a much larger army than Caesar's in Greece, North Africa and Spain. The war spread through all those countries.

The biggest battle took place at Pharsalus in Greece. Pompey's army was twice the size of Caesar's and well-defended in a walled fortress. For three days Caesar's army paraded in front of Pompey's fortress, trying to tempt him out. On the fourth day, Pompey marched out at the head of his forces. Caesar charged with his infantry and Pompey counter-attacked with his cavalry. A bloodbath followed. Pompey started to pull back and Caesar's cavalry followed them, showing no mercy.

## WHO WON IN THE END?

Pompey entered the battle of Pharsalus in 48 BC with 45,000 men. At the end of the battle, 15,000 of them lay dead and thousands more were wounded or captured. Pompey himself escaped and disappeared for seven weeks. When he turned up in Egypt he was promptly murdered by one of Caesar's supporters.

*It was said that on the opposite bank Caesar saw a giant ghostly figure. The strange figure took hold of a trumpet, blew it and led his followers over the river.*

# SUPREME AT LAST!

He had absolute power over Rome and its vast empire. In 44 BC he was given the title of Dictator for Life which meant that he had complete control of all the offices of government, the Roman treasury and all the Roman armies. He could even pass laws, which up to then had to be voted on by the people. No Roman had ever been so powerful.

*Lion killing a man in the Roman circus (see below). Caesar laid on a huge programme of entertainments, including one which involved the slaughter of over four hundred lions.*

## HOW DID HE BEHAVE WHEN HE TOOK POWER?

He wanted to be popular and secure. One of the first things he did was give a massive banquet for 20,000 poor people. At the end each guest received a take-home present of money, grain and oil. He very generously forgave his enemies, even those who had supported Pompey. Many good and useful men had been on Pompey's side and Caesar wanted to win them back. Caesar was thought to be unusually merciful to his Roman enemies throughout his career.

## WHAT CHANGES DID HE MAKE?

CITIZENSHIP LAW: The special privilege of being a Roman citizen who could vote in elections and enjoy the full protection of the law was extended to everybody living within the Roman Empire – except slaves and women of course.

TRAFFIC: Rome had appalling traffic problems. Caesar solved it by banning all heavy goods traffic from the streets except at night.

*Carriages and carts such as these crowded the narrow streets of Rome. Sometimes the whole central area got completely jammed up.*

*The inscription on this slave tag reads, 'Hold me, lest I flee, and return me to my master Viventius on the estate of Callistus'.*

## DID HE RULE WELL?

He certainly kept good order and passed some sensible laws. But he destroyed some of the old systems that Romans had been proud of. Until then laws had been openly debated and voted on in the assembly so that they were seen to be fair and wise. Caesar now made laws himself and people had to vote the way he told them.

### THE CALENDAR

He reformed the old very complicated calendar. His new system divided the year into our modern three hundred and sixty-five days with four-yearly leap days. Due to the changeover 46 BC was the longest year in history with 445 days.

*Caesar's arrival back in Rome after his defeat of Pompey and his followers was celebrated by a series of huge processions or Triumphs.*

His most famous saying, Veni, vide, vici, – 'I came, I saw, I conquered' *was inscribed on a banner carried at one of these Triumphs.*

# TOO MUCH PRIDE? TOO MUCH POWER?

Most Romans hated the idea of kings. Far back in history they had expelled their kings and did not want them back. Rome was now a Republic. This meant that all laws had to be voted on and nobody could hold high positions unless they had been elected. This is what many Romans wanted to preserve – but Caesar was gradually destroying this system.

## WAS CAESAR PLANNING TO BE KING?

Even his close friends were beginning to think that Caesar was becoming dangerously proud. He did things that were bound to worry them. For example, he had his own statue placed beside the statues of the ancient kings of Rome. He also set up his own statue in a temple and inscribed on it 'To the Unconquerable God'. He sat on a magnificent gold throne and held an ivory sceptre. He wore every day the beautiful robes that normally were worn only by heroes in a Triumph.

The leading Roman citizens had good reasons to be concerned. It looked as though Caesar wanted to make himself king.

*Caesar even had his own head placed on the Roman coins, which nobody had done before.*

Rome was full of rumours (left). It was even being said that Caesar intended to move the government to Egypt. After all, he had installed Cleopatra, Queen of Egypt, and their son, Caesarion, in his villa in Rome.

On this coin a citizen is seen casting his voting tablet into the urn.

## THE SECRET BALLOT

*One of the Romans' most prized liberties was the Secret Ballot. Each voter would receive his voting tablet from an election officer. Barriers separated him from other voters and there was a narrow raised walk to ensure he cast his vote freely, without influence.*

Caesar had his own statue placed beside the statues of the ancient kings of Rome.

Caesar set up a golden statue of Cleopatra (left), in his new temple for Venus, the goddess of love. Many Romans feared he might even marry her.

### WHAT WAS THE ARGUMENT IN FAVOUR OF MAKING HIM KING?

The old Republican system was not working well. Politicians bribed and bullied their way to power and fought among themselves. One simple solution would be to end the voting system and all the corruption. Crown Caesar king and let him do things his way.

# BEWARE THE IDES OF MARCH!

Caesar had many secret enemies, men who were worried that he was far too powerful. He was uneasy. He didn't know exactly who to fear – but there was one thin-faced man called Cassius that he didn't trust.

*Temple sacrifice (below). Caesar's murder made a big impression on Roman historians. They described magic signs foretelling his death such as the sacrifice of an animal with no heart.*

**DANGER AHEAD?**

In those days the Romans believed in magic signs or omens that told the future. People started spreading rumours of frightening omens around the city. Weird spirits had been seen running through the night. Caesar, sacrificing an animal in the temple, found that it had no heart! Then another frightening thing happened. As he was walking through the city a fortune teller called out in a horrible voice, 'Beware the Ides of March!' The Ides of March was the 15th of the month – which was quite soon. On the night of the Ides of March, there was a terrible wind blowing through the city. Everybody felt unsettled.

*A Roman calendar (below). Our names of the months still retain their Roman origins, such as January, for Janus, god of beginnings and endings and March, for Mars, god of war.*

## WAS THERE A PLOT BREWING?

The mysterious warnings of the Ides of March were true. There was a plot to murder Caesar. A group of very senior politicians had made up their minds to get rid of their overpowerful dictator on March 15, 44 BC.

As many as sixty men were in the plot. We often refer to them as the Conspirators. They were not evil men. They believed that they were acting for the good of Rome. They included a very distinguished senator called Marcus Brutus, the son of Caesar's old girlfriend, Servilia. He had been one of Caesar's trusted friends. And also thin-faced Cassius.

## DID CAESAR FEAR DEATH?

Friends warned Caesar that he should provide himself with another body-guard, but he refused. Nothing he said was more miserable than having oneself guarded. Only someone who was always afraid needed that. He told a friend that, 'it was better to die than always to be afraid of death'.

*As a soldier, Caesar had never shown fear. Now, as a middle-aged politician, he still refused to be protected by special bodyguards.*

# MURDER MOST FOUL!

The Conspirators wanted to carry out their murder in public so that everybody should witness what they had done.

**WHAT WAS THE PLAN?**

They chose the Senate House, which is where the leading politicians had, for hundreds of years, met to pass laws and vote on important issues. They knew that Caesar was due to come down from his palace to the Senate at a particular time. Twenty-three of the Conspirators were in the Senate and each carried a hidden dagger. They all wanted to have an equal share in the murder; they would deliver twenty-three stabs.

Caesar arrived rather later than usual. He was surrounded by the usual crowd of people trying to get his attention with various petitions and requests.

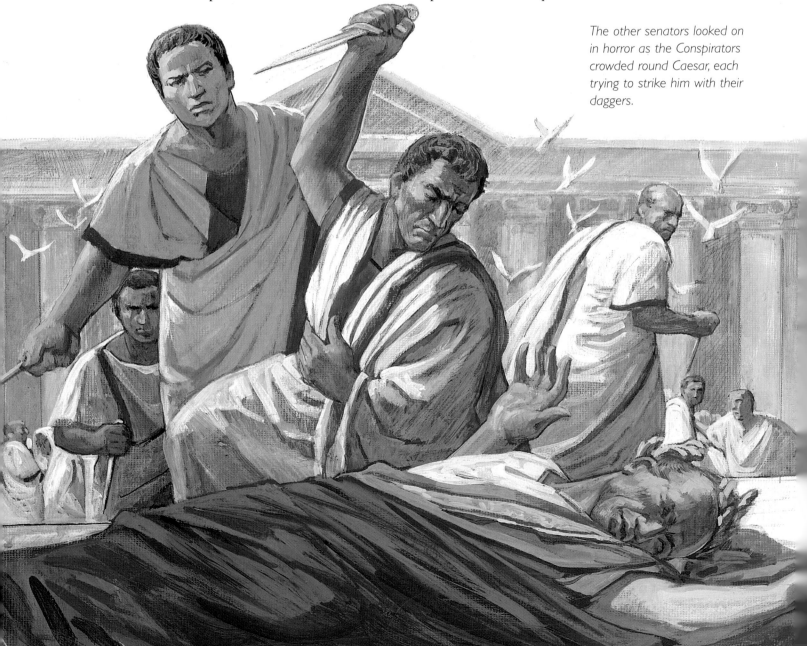

*The other senators looked on in horror as the Conspirators crowded round Caesar, each trying to strike him with their daggers.*

## HOW DID THEY KILL CAESAR?

The Conspirators waited for Caesar to sit on his throne in front of all the senators. Then one of them, called Metellus, pulled his cloak down over his neck – which was the signal to the others to form a circle round Caesar. They drew their daggers.

The first blow to the neck was made by a man called Casca who had done most of the planning for the murder. It didn't go deep and Caesar wheeled round, caught Casca's arm and ran it through with the stylus he used for writing. Then all of the Conspirators crowded round Caesar, each trying to strike him with their daggers. Caesar struggled to get free until he met the gaze of Brutus.

'You too, Brutus?' he gasped as Brutus struck the final blow. In his last moments, he pulled his toga over his head so that nobody would see him die.

*Brutus (left) genuinely believed in republican ideals, which is why he became a leading Conspirator.*

*Behind Caesar's dead body stood the statue of his old enemy, Pompey (above), now splattered with blood.*

## WERE THE CONSPIRATORS AFRAID?

The Conspirators were not frightened. They bravely walked through the crowd carrying their blood-stained daggers and stood in the main square to explain what they had done. Brutus gave a magnificent speech telling people that they had been saved from a tyrant.

*A coin commemorating the Ides of March, which was issued by Brutus's army later on. These coins would have been used to pay the soldiers.*

# THE AFTERMATH OF CAESAR'S MURDER

There was no obvious choice of new leader after Julius Caesar's death. Instead, far from ensuring the return of the Republic, as the Conspirators had hoped, his death led to an appalling period of anarchy and civil war.

**HOW DID THE PEOPLE REACT TO THE MURDER?**

The citizens of Rome were horrified by the murder. Some fled to their own houses and stayed there in case there was more violence. Others ran out into the street to see what was going on. All were in confusion. No one knew who was in charge.

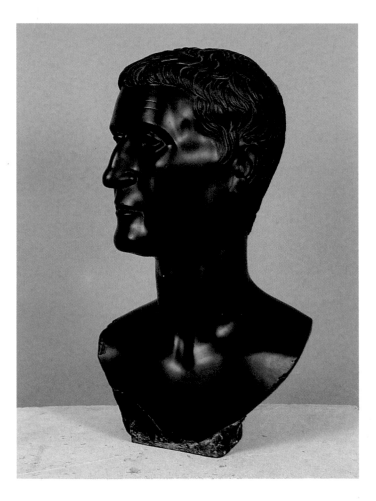

**WHAT HAPPENED AT HIS FUNERAL?**

Caesar's body was brought out in a huge funeral procession and laid in the city centre. His close friend, Mark Antony held up the blood-stained toga with its twenty-three holes and gave a rousing speech bewailing the death of their great ruler.

When they heard this, the crowd went wild. Some ran through the city carrying burning torches in search of the murderers, planning to tear them to pieces. But the Conspirators had wisely hidden.

The main crowd decided to show their gratitude to Caesar by making a huge fire in the middle of the forum to burn his body on. They gathered firewood, furniture, even the doors of houses, to make a great pyre. Amidst wailing and cries, the body of the greatest Roman of them all was reduced to ashes.

*Mark Antony (left). Caesar's second-in-command, fought alongside Caesar in Gaul and in the Civil War. He was always a loyal friend.*

*Amidst wailing and cries, the body of the greatest Roman of them all was to be reduced to ashes (right).*

## HOW DID IT ALL END?

In the Civil War that followed Caesar's death, Brutus and Cassius were defeated by Mark Antony and Caesar's great nephew, Octavian, at the battle of Philippi in Greece in 42 BC. Brutus and Cassius committed suicide after the battle.

*Octavian, Caesar's own great-nephew, adopted by him as his son and heir.*

Two great rivals were left to fight each other for power: Octavian and Mark Antony, who had rather spoilt his chances by falling in love with Cleopatra. An enormous sea battle took place between them at Actium in 31 BC. Octavian won and Antony and Cleopatra committed suicide.

There was at last peace. Octavian, Caesar's chosen heir, was now all-powerful. He became Rome's first Emperor in 27 BC, calling himself Augustus Caesar. This was close to what Julius Caesar had striven for and what Brutus and his friends had most dreaded.

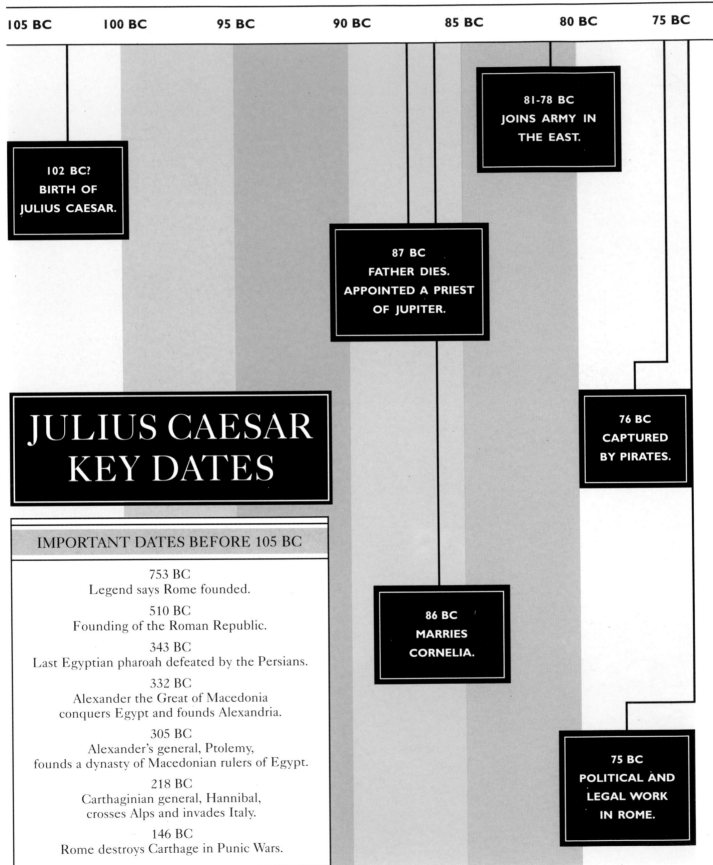

| 105 BC | 100 BC | 95 BC | 90 BC | 85 BC | 80 BC | 75 BC |
|---|---|---|---|---|---|---|

**81–78 BC JOINS ARMY IN THE EAST.**

**102 BC? BIRTH OF JULIUS CAESAR.**

**87 BC FATHER DIES. APPOINTED A PRIEST OF JUPITER.**

**76 BC CAPTURED BY PIRATES.**

# JULIUS CAESAR KEY DATES

## IMPORTANT DATES BEFORE 105 BC

753 BC
Legend says Rome founded.

510 BC
Founding of the Roman Republic.

343 BC
Last Egyptian pharoah defeated by the Persians.

332 BC
Alexander the Great of Macedonia
conquers Egypt and founds Alexandria.

305 BC
Alexander's general, Ptolemy,
founds a dynasty of Macedonian rulers of Egypt.

218 BC
Carthaginian general, Hannibal,
crosses Alps and invades Italy.

146 BC
Rome destroys Carthage in Punic Wars.

**86 BC MARRIES CORNELIA.**

**75 BC POLITICAL AND LEGAL WORK IN ROME.**

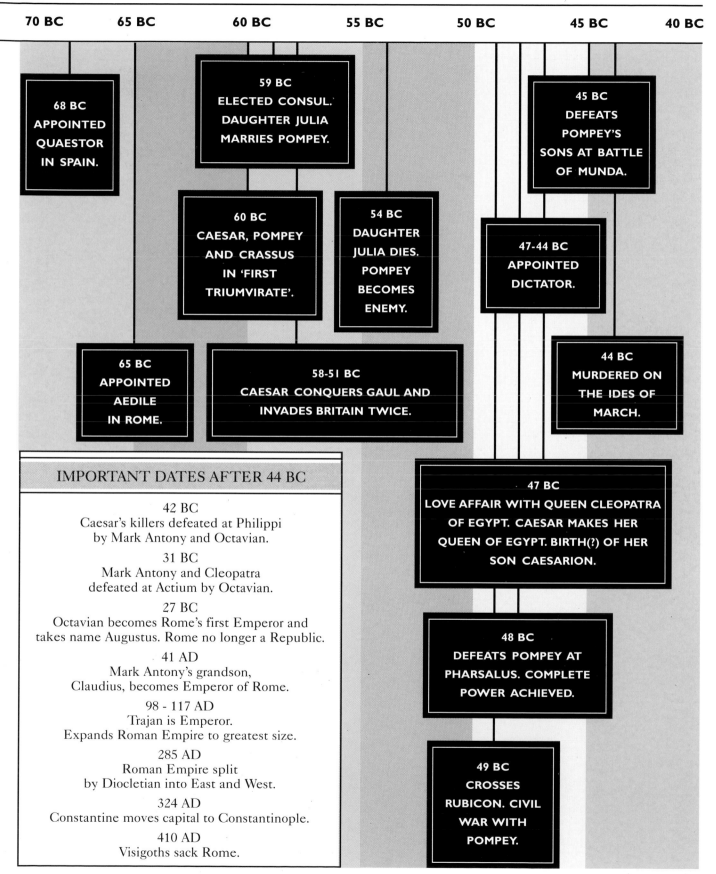

| 70 BC | 65 BC | 60 BC | 55 BC | 50 BC | 45 BC | 40 BC |
|-------|-------|-------|-------|-------|-------|-------|

**68 BC**
APPOINTED QUAESTOR IN SPAIN.

**59 BC**
ELECTED CONSUL. DAUGHTER JULIA MARRIES POMPEY.

**45 BC**
DEFEATS POMPEY'S SONS AT BATTLE OF MUNDA.

**60 BC**
CAESAR, POMPEY AND CRASSUS IN 'FIRST TRIUMVIRATE'.

**54 BC**
DAUGHTER JULIA DIES. POMPEY BECOMES ENEMY.

**47-44 BC**
APPOINTED DICTATOR.

**65 BC**
APPOINTED AEDILE IN ROME.

**58-51 BC**
CAESAR CONQUERS GAUL AND INVADES BRITAIN TWICE.

**44 BC**
MURDERED ON THE IDES OF MARCH.

**47 BC**
LOVE AFFAIR WITH QUEEN CLEOPATRA OF EGYPT. CAESAR MAKES HER QUEEN OF EGYPT. BIRTH(?) OF HER SON CAESARION.

**48 BC**
DEFEATS POMPEY AT PHARSALUS. COMPLETE POWER ACHIEVED.

**49 BC**
CROSSES RUBICON. CIVIL WAR WITH POMPEY.

## IMPORTANT DATES AFTER 44 BC

**42 BC**
Caesar's killers defeated at Philippi by Mark Antony and Octavian.

**31 BC**
Mark Antony and Cleopatra defeated at Actium by Octavian.

**27 BC**
Octavian becomes Rome's first Emperor and takes name Augustus. Rome no longer a Republic.

**41 AD**
Mark Antony's grandson, Claudius, becomes Emperor of Rome.

**98 - 117 AD**
Trajan is Emperor. Expands Roman Empire to greatest size.

**285 AD**
Roman Empire split by Diocletian into East and West.

**324 AD**
Constantine moves capital to Constantinople.

**410 AD**
Visigoths sack Rome.

# GLOSSARY

AEDILE  He had the job of looking after public events, buildings and the state archives.

CITIZEN  A person with the right to vote in elections and be protected by Roman law. (This of course excluded slaves. And women could not vote.)

CIVIL WAR  War between two sections of a nation. The Romans had several civil wars, including that between Caesar and Pompey.

CONSULS  Two very senior officials elected annually to control the army in Rome and oversee the administration. Caesar first became a consul briefly in 59 BC.

DICTATOR  In Rome, a ruler given complete and absolute power in times of national danger. Caesar was given the title of Dictator for Life, which had never happened before.

GALLEY  Warship, usually rowed by slaves, carrying armed soldiers. Caesar had some built specially to invade Britain.

GLADIATORS  Men, usually prisoners or slaves, who were forced to fight each other in public to entertain spectators. Caesar owned several hundred gladiators.

IDES  In the ancient Roman calendar, the 15th day of March, May, July, and October, and the 13th of the other months.

LATIN  Language spoken and written by the Romans.

LEGION  A unit of about 6,000 soldiers, all of them full Roman citizens, serving for 20 years.

OMEN  A strange event or sign that people believed foretold the future. Many omens were reported before Caesar's murder.

REPUBLIC  A system of government which does not have a king. Rulers are normally elected by the citizens. The Roman Republic finally came to an end after Caesar's death.

RHETORIC  The art of speaking in public. Caesar continued to have rhetoric lessons long after he had grown up.

SENATE  An assembly of leading Roman citizens, usually former senior officials, who met in a building called the Curia to propose new laws and oversee the government of Rome.

SLAVES  Men or women who could be bought, sold and punished by their owner. They usually did the rough work in the house or on the farm but some were well-educated and became tutors, secretaries and even doctors.

PATRICIANS  Upper class of Roman society.

PLEBEIANS  Name given to working people.

PRAETORS  They were the highest level of magistrates in Roman courts of law.

TOGA  The national dress for Roman men. Worn over a tunic, it was a semi-circle piece of cloth that had to be draped round the body from the shoulders. The toga for citizens had to be pure white.

TRIBUNE  Officer in a Roman legion.

TRIUMPH  A parade held to celebrate the return to Rome of a victorious general.

VENUS  The Roman goddess of love and beauty. Caesar built her a temple in Rome because he claimed to be a descendant of hers.

# INDEX

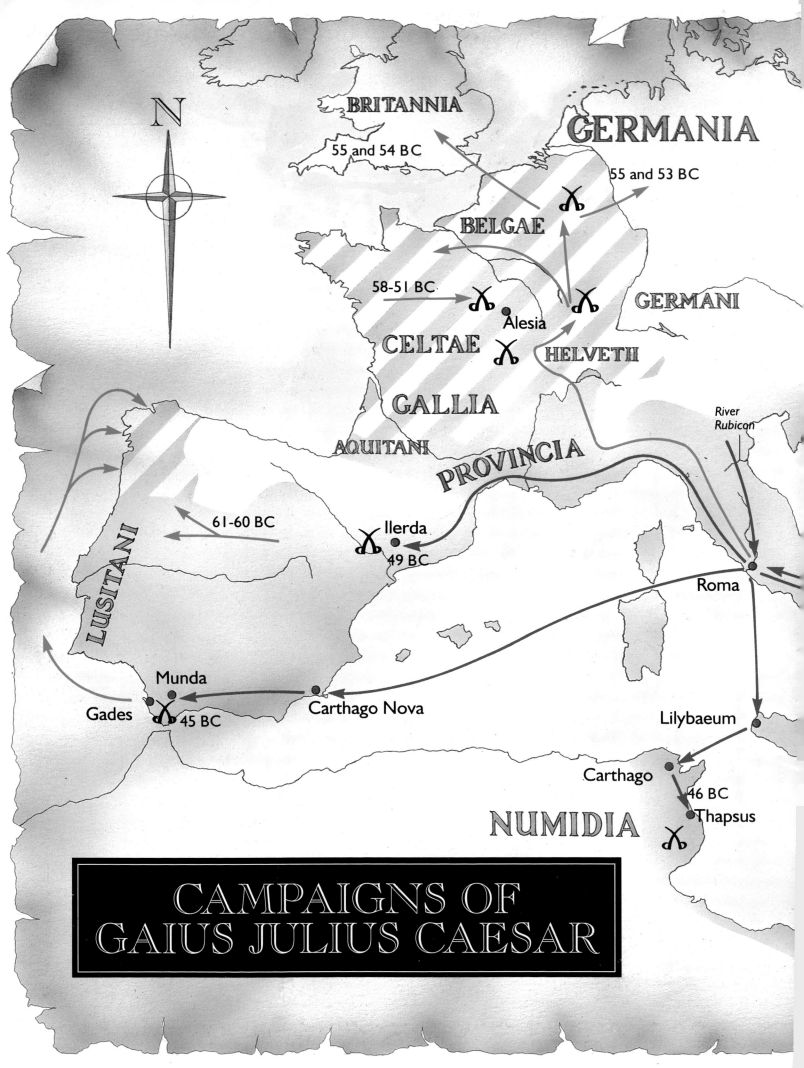

# CAMPAIGNS OF GAIUS JULIUS CAESAR